MW01626272
dragonflies soaring
rabbits hopping
turtles sunning
rickets chirping
children playing

Butterfly Birthday

Butterfly Birthday

written and illustrated by

Lori Stralow Harris

The Wooster Book Company

where minds and imaginatons meet

Wooster Ohio ✣ 2016

The Wooster Book Company
205 West Liberty Street
Wooster, Ohio 44691
www.wooster book.com

ISBN: 978-1-59098-588-5

Second Printing
Printed and bound in the United States of America on acid-free paper.
3 5 7 9 10 8 6 4 2

The illustrations in this book were done with pastels.
The text of this book is set in Goudy Old Style.

This book is dedicated to
Nate and Marni,
whose bare little feet carried them on many exciting backyard adventures –
and to Mark,
who encourages me to still seek out adventures of my own.

Just down the road, not far away,

Is a patch full of weeds where butterflies play.

Soft, gentle wings flitting flower to flower,

Tongues sipping nectar, hour after hour.

If you're quiet and patient, and stand very still

Most *never see it* – *but maybe* you *will*.

The mammas touch down, one at a time,

To lay eggs on a leaf, or a stem, or a vine.

Several days later, from out of the eggs,

March itty, bitty caterpillars with short, little legs.

They parade up and down, and put on a show.

Chewing on leaves, they grow …

and they GROW!

When they've grown big enough
and have gotten quite plump,
They dance and they wiggle,
they twist and then scrunch.

The change is surprising –

if you're lucky you'll see …

It's hard to describe –

it's hard to believe!

By scrunching their bodies
from their heads to their toes,
They take off their patterns
like you'd take off your clothes!

Then they get very quiet –
like they're going to sleep,
Not for a night, but a couple of weeks.

These shapes seem the same,
day after day,
They don't eat, they don't move.
They surely don't play!

But inside they're changing –
they're very alive!
They're just rearranging,
getting ready to fly.

Then finally one morning –
please don't look away,
Oh, I hope you can see it…

It's a Butterfly Birthday!

Monarchs ready for release at Salt Creek Butterfly Farm

One of the most rewarding experiences you can share with a child is raising and releasing a butterfly into the wild.

Lori Harris opened Salt Creek Butterfly Farm in 2012 to inspire her community to slow down and observe the patterns and rhythms of life present in our own backyards.

Salt Creek Butterfly Farm gives away thousands of butterfly eggs each summer to friends, neighbors, schools, and organizations throughout the greater Chicago area.

If you would like to find a butterfly egg, feed a caterpillar, marvel at the gentle form of a chrysalis, or be surprised by the full-sized butterfly that emerges from it, visit the Salt Creek Butterfly Farm website for more information.

www.saltcreekbutterflyfarm.com

Butterfly Birthdays happen every day and ***You're Invited!***

bluebirds nesting
toads croaking
butterflies flitting
bees buzzing